D0746486

Someday

Someday

A Play by
Drew Hayden Taylor

FIFTH
HOUSE
PUBLISHERS

Copyright © 1993 by Drew Hayden Taylor

All rights reserved. No part of this publication may be reproduced
in any form or by any means without the prior written permission
of the publisher, except in the case of a reviewer, who may quote
brief passages in a review to print in a magazine or newspaper, or
broadcast on radio or television. In the case of photocopying or other
reprographic copying, users must obtain a licence from the Canadian
Copyright Licensing Agency. Permission to perform the play, in whole
or in part, must be obtained from the author, c/o the publisher.

Cover design by John Luckhurst/GDL
Cover photograph of the author by Sherry Huff

The publisher gratefully acknowledges the support
received from The Canada Council and Heritage Canada.

Printed and bound in Canada by Friesens, Altona, MB
15 / 8

All characters and events in *Someday* are fictional.

CANADIAN CATALOGUING IN PUBLICATION DATA
Taylor, Drew Hayden, 1962–

Someday

A play.
ISBN 1-895618-10-X

I. Title.

PS8589.A885S6 1993   C812'.54   C92-098172-0
PR9199.3.T295S6   1993

FIFTH HOUSE LTD.

*To all the people
who are looking,
and all the people
who are waiting.*

Acknowledgements

The original concept and story line for *Someday* came from a story I wrote for *The Globe and Mail*. It was published as the *Globe*'s annual Christmas short story on 24 December 1990. I'm told it was the first piece of (intentional) fiction ever published on the front page.

And may whoever watches us from above look down and bless Larry Lewis for recognizing the dramatic possibilities of the piece and having the idea of turning it into a play.

A special thanks to the Banff Playwright Colony for providing me with the opportunity of fleshing out the story and coming away with a workable first draft.

Someday was produced by De-ba-jeh-mu-jig Theatre Group, located on Manitoulin Island. It premiered on 4 November 1991 at the Wikwemikong Reserve, Ontario, with what I consider a dream cast and crew.

> Herbie Barnes . . . Rodney
> Joy Keeper . . . Barb
> Edna Manitowabi . . . Anne
> Doris Linklater . . . Grace/Janice
> Directed by Larry Lewis, with Floyd Favel
> Lights and sets by Stephen Droege
> Music by Marsha Coffey
> Stage managed by Sheila Kinoshameg

There are many other people I would like to thank who in some way provided support or encouragement for this small piece of theatre: Audrey Debassige, Kait Mathews, Maxine Noel, Fuddy Fisher, Zeke Peltier, The Toronto Native Child and Family Services, Sonny Osawabine, Laurie Baldhead, and everybody else at De-ba-jeh-mu-jig Theatre that I haven't mentioned.

Cast of Characters

Rodney, 25, friend of the family
Barb Wabung, 23, Rodney's girlfriend
Anne Wabung, 53, mother of Barb and Janice
Janice (Grace) Wirth, 35, the long-lost daughter/sister

Location

This play takes place in a fictional Ojibway community on the Otter Lake Reserve, somewhere in central Ontario. It could also take place in any Native community in Canada.

Time

The last week before Christmas 1991—a time of great happiness and sadness.

Life:
The Creator's Way of Saying
"Impress Me"

Act I

It is the week before Christmas on the Otter Lake Reserve. Rodney, an Ojibway man of 25, is shovelling snow. Behind him, boasting a big picture window looking into a homey, well-equipped if modestly appointed country kitchen, is a pre-turn-of-the-century frame house with a near dangerous physical lean to the left. The building is decorated with Christmas regalia. Rodney is singing but is enjoying nothing. The sound of Christmas carols can be heard in the background.

RODNEY:
> "'Tis the season to be jolly (*raspberries*), thppth, thppth, thppth, thppth, thppth . . . thppth, thppth, thppth, thppth." God, I hate Christmas. I really do. I hate the way everything gets speeded up two extra notches, like diarrhoea after bad cranberry sauce. I hate all the distant relatives who treat you like you just gave them a kidney. Greedy kids, greedy adults, greedy department stores. I hate those stupid songs: the bad Frosties and Rudolphs; 'twas the night before Christmas with mice of all things; The Flintstones meet Santa Claus; Gilligan's Island meets Santa Claus; and in 1969 even the Apollo astronauts meet Santa Claus. And most of all, I hate snow. The more you shovel, the more seems to come, like homework. I came back home for this? At least in the city they pay white people to do this. The ironic thing is, this isn't even my driveway. That makes me more miserable. Snow to the left of me. Snow to the right of me. My kingdom for a snowblower!

Barb, 23, walks on carrying shopping bags full of Christmas-type materials, wrapping paper, ribbons, etc.

BARB:
Waiting for the snow to melt?

RODNEY:
I'm waiting for my heart to restart, if you must know.

BARB:
Quit slacking off. Try to finish the driveway before dark, huh?

RODNEY:
And while I have the shovel, a new foundation for a house perhaps?

BARB:
Don't bother, that would take a man, with muscles.

RODNEY:
Oh, your wit skewers me.

BARB:
Whatever.

Barb leaves the driveway and enters the house. A Chipmunks Christmas carol commences to play.

RODNEY:
Ah yes, the Chipmunks. The voice of sanity in this depressingly cheery season. And that ravishing creature was my little speedbump on the road of happiness. The girl of my dreams—or sometimes nightmares. I'm told we have a peculiar relationship, sort of like a cross between Oka and a cheap motel: we fight, we make up, we make love, we fight again. Sometimes we fight while making love. If it wasn't for the luxurious job she enjoys at the band office, it just wouldn't be the same. We'd be broke.

Anne, a woman in her mid-50s, enters. She is carrying containers, some empty, others filled with various leather and beaded crafts.

ANNE:
Hey there, handsome. How's the job going?

RODNEY:
With a job you get paid.

ANNE:
I don't know what your usual fee is but how's about a good old-fashioned cookie?

She pries open a Tupperware container and offers Rodney a cookie. Rodney takes it.

RODNEY:
Ooh, chocolate chip.

ANNE:
It's all I need in life. My chocolate chip cookies, my soap operas, and my lottery tickets. What else is there? Someday I'm gonna be rich. Just you wait.

Rodney watches as Anne enters the house.

RODNEY:
Anne. I think she's one of the reasons I put up with Barb. There's just the two of them now. The Wabungs, mother and daughter, oil and vinegar, salt and pepper, cats and dogs. Well, you know what I mean. (*he walks up to the house*) It's amazing this house is still standing. If you'll notice, there is a definite lean to the left. (*he points*) Because of that, I like to call it the Communist House. Get it, lean to the left? Anne is convinced the house will outlive her and Barb. "People die, but never memories." And this place is full of memories. Every family has their skeletons. The Wabungs are no different.

Rodney looks towards the house. Anne and Barb can be seen in silhouette through the big window as they move back and forth.

RODNEY:
Kind of looks like a big television set, don't it? Or a

movie screen. Oh, the drama of it all. Me, I just cruise through reality, have a good time, sing a little song, dance a little dance. It's a rough life. Anyways, back to the salt mines. (*he shovels snow*) I love her. (*shovel*) I hate her. (*shovel*) I love her. (*shovel*) I hate her. (*shovel*) They don't even own a car.

Barb screams from within the house.

BARB:
Rodney! Rodney! Come quick! Hurry!

Rodney drops his shovel and races for the porch. He stops, considers. Then he runs back, picks up the shovel, and races into the house brandishing it like a weapon.

RODNEY:
What? What is it? A mouse? A bat? What? Where?

Anne is sitting at the table, the newspaper spread out in front of her. She coughs slightly. Barb is backed up against the counter, her hands in front of her mouth. She has a very stunned look on her face.

RODNEY:
Anne, are you okay? Is it your heart? Oh, my God, it's your heart. I'll call 911.

He races for the telephone. Barb goes to him quickly and grabs his shirt sleeve. She grunts.

RODNEY:
This is no time for love talk.

Barb grunts twice, passionately. She points towards the table.

RODNEY:
What?!

She hauls him over to the table. Anne points to the paper with one finger. Rodney squints over it.

RODNEY:
> The lottery numbers. Yeah? So?

Anne holds up her lottery ticket in her other hand. Confused, Rodney looks at it. Suddenly it begins to dawn on him. He looks back and forth at the ticket and paper several times before throwing himself against the refrigerator with the exact same expression Barb had. They are all silent for a moment.

RODNEY:
> Did that say five hundred thousand dollars?

BARB:
> No. Five million.

Rodney screams at the top of his lungs. Barb screams in staccato bursts, and Anne jumps up and screams a healthy and wonderful blast.

ANNE:
> This proves to all you nonbelievers that there is a God. And more importantly, He likes me. He likes me five million times! Oh, what a glorious Christmas!

BARB:
> Five million dollars! Five million dollars! Do you know what this means? I can kiss the band office goodbye. Adiós, buenas noches, sayonara suckers.

Anne is shocked at Barb's rudeness.

ANNE:
> Barb!

BARB:
> What? We can retire.

ANNE:
> You're 23. What are you gonna do for the rest of your life, fish for 50 years?

BARB:
> Hey, I can handle that. Why? What do you wanna do with it?

ANNE:
> Well, I thought maybe we could get some new screens for the porch. They're looking kind of ratty. Maybe build an extension on this place.

BARB:
> A rec room?

ANNE:
> A sewing room.

BARB:
> That's all?

ANNE:
> Maybe a new dress.

BARB:
> Think bigger, Mom.

ANNE:
> Two dresses?

RODNEY:
> Is the word "invest" in either of your vocabularies?

Barb dismisses Rodney.

BARB:
> Oh, right, I'm taking financial advice from *you*.

RODNEY:
> Hey, so I've had a financial setback.

BARB:
> The band cut off your funding. You can't be a professional student forever.

Barb and Rodney start to argue but Anne cuts them off.

ANNE:
Will you two cut it out? You're acting like a couple of dogs. Do you really think we should invest it, Rodney?

RODNEY:
Definitely. As they say, we'll make the money work for us.

Barb looks at him quizzically.

BARB:
What's this "us" business?

RODNEY:
Well, I thought . . . You know . . . You still like me, don't you?

BARB:
Think again. Hit the road, Shorty.

ANNE:
Barb! You apologize to him right now.

BARB:
I was only kidding. He knows that, don't you, Rodney?

Rodney remains unconvinced. He watches her warily.

RODNEY:
Yeah, I guess.

Anne is looking off at a picture on the wall, but the other two are oblivious.

BARB:
How do we claim the money?

RODNEY:
Go to the lottery office in Toronto, show them the ticket, and you'll get your money. I think.

BARB:

We better take every suitcase. Think we can get the
money in 10s and 20s?

RODNEY:

Five million dollars in cash in those small suitcases?

BARB:

You're right. Better take some garbage bags.

RODNEY:

I think they give you a cheque.

BARB:

A cheque?

RODNEY:

Yep.

BARB:

Then we'll only need one suitcase. If we leave now, we
could be there before seven.

RODNEY:

The office would be closed.

BARB:

You don't think they would stay open for two of
Canada's newest millionaires? We'll tip.

RODNEY:

Calm down. The ticket isn't going anywhere. I'll borrow
my brother's car tomorrow and take you in myself.
How's that?

Rational talk has no effect on Barb.

BARB:

I wanna go now! There's five million dollars waiting
for us with our name on every single one. Quit stalling.
I hate collecting dusty money.

RODNEY:
Geez, take it easy. It's not going anywhere.

BARB:
You sure?

RODNEY:
You've got the ticket. Who'd take it?

BARB:
The government?

RODNEY:
Come on, Barb, what's one more Kraft dinner? You can almost make it now without reading the box.

ANNE:
Rodney, do you think it's possible for dreams to come true? I mean really possible?

BARB:
Of course they can come true. Mine just did.

ANNE:
I only have one dream.

Anne gets up and walks over to the wall where there is a small black-and-white photograph. She looks at it wistfully.

RODNEY:
What dream is that, Anne?

Barb elbows him in the ribs. The mood in the room becomes downbeat.

BARB:
Don't get her started. I hate it when she puts herself through this. They took her away a long time ago, Mom. For all we know she could be dead.

Anne wheels around and slaps Barb's face. Tension is heavy in the air.

ANNE:
> Don't you ever say that. Don't you ever say that again. She's alive. I know she is. In here (*points to her heart*) and out there. I want my baby back. We can use this money to hire one of them private detectives to track her down. You talk about her like she wasn't a part of this family. She was a part of this family before you were even born. She's your older sister. Why do you think the money came now? It's a gift from God, His way of telling me He wants us to be a family again. We're going to have a happy Christmas, a Christmas to remember. And I won't hear you talking contrary.

Barb is still rubbing her cheek. Anne starts to put on her sweater and dresses herself during the following dialogue for a trek outdoors.

BARB:
> You hit me.

ANNE:
> And I'd do it again.

BARB:
> You never hit me before.

ANNE:
> I never wanted to before.

BARB:
> Where are you going?

ANNE:
> No place you need worry yourself about. It doesn't concern a girl who don't care and I'll tell you this right now, never . . . *never* in my entire life did I expect to see a daughter of mine bad mouth her own flesh and blood.

BARB:
Stop taking it out on me. Just stop. It's not my fault.

Rodney reaches for his jacket.

RODNEY:
Well, I can see I'm probably embarrassing you two by being here, this obviously being a family matter.

BARB:
Rodney, sit down. (*to Anne*) You gotta stop blaming yourself for what happened sometime, Mom. You gotta let things go. Look at Agnes Weasel, she's been waiting for over 40 years for her son to come back. Nobody remembers if he even existed, but she still sits there, waiting. That's the only thing that keeps her alive. A shell of a woman waiting by her window. I don't want that for you. Grace is the past. I've lived in her shadow for 23 years. Enough is enough.

ANNE:
You weren't in anybody's shadow, except in your own mind. You are my youngest, my baby. You are so close to my heart, you are my heart.

Rodney is definitely ill at ease, wishing he weren't there. Anne starts to put her jacket on.

BARB:
Will you tell me where you're going, please?

ANNE:
To the band office before they close up. They have a Toronto phone book. Somewhere in those dandelion-coloured pages is the man who might just find my daughter. Do you have anything to say about that?

Anne's look is one of challenge.

BARB:
Yeah. (*pause*) I'll get my coat.

*Barb kisses Rodney quickly and leads her mother outside
and off down the road.*

RODNEY:
> You know, this place is almost 100 years old. The band
> has offered to build Anne a new one any time she wants,
> and I've told her, "take it." But no. "I was born here, I
> had my kids here, and I'll die here." Getting her out of
> this house is one thing, but it takes a hell of a lot to drag
> Anne out of this village, and God bless her, there she
> was in downtown Toronto. (*as Rodney talks, a light
> comes up on Anne and Barb as they appear and mime
> their trip to Toronto*) Posing for camera after camera,
> smile after smile till the energy drifted out of those
> cheeks and was replaced by a tired grimace. Hands to
> shake, people to wave at, questions to answer. Then
> came the fabled cheque. Barb swears up and down she
> saw it quiver when Anne touched it. Then of course
> there were windows to shop, stores to drool over,
> dreams to price. "I want that, and that, and we could get
> that, I could lose weight and get that." It was a 50/50
> split, Barb's window shopping and Anne's detective
> shopping. None of us knew what a real detective looked
> like other than from television, but by the end of the
> day, there would be no more staying up on Friday nights
> to watch "Magnum P.I." We had detective overload. On
> our way back to the car, we passed a drunk on the
> street. Anne stopped and watched the poor woman for a
> moment, as if trying to find the image of a seven-month-
> old baby in her rough face. Anne walked up to the needy
> woman and gave her 20 dollars. I thought that was kinda
> sweet, then I realized that was our gas money. We barely
> made it home on fumes. Let's see you try and cash a five-
> million-dollar cheque at a gas station.

*Rodney opens the door and is starting to walk through when
he is pushed aside by Barb.*

BARB:
> Will you hurry up? It's cold out there and I've had to pee
> since Whitby.

Barb hurries on her way to the bathroom, doing a sort of
rapid, pigeon-toed "I gotta pee" walk. Anne enters, followed
by Rodney. She turns the thermostat up and fills the kettle.

ANNE:
> Tea, I need tea. Rodney?

RODNEY:
> Yes, please.

ANNE:
> All them reporters, cameras. I've never shaken so many
> hands. *(holds up her hand)* It feels like five pieces of spa-
> ghetti. You'd think Indians never won anything before.
> Can you imagine the nerve of the chief flagging us down
> this morning to try and borrow some money? Twelve
> years ago when Frank was a councillor and still alive I
> begged him to talk to the chief about getting our peoples'
> kids back from the Children's Aid Society, but Frank just
> got mad. "Let sleeping dogs lie" was all he said, rest his
> soul, and I said my Grace wasn't a dog, she was my baby.
> "She's somebody else's now. She's dead to us, Anne. Let
> her rest." Dead to us. I went behind his back and spoke to
> the chief myself. Wouldn't do nothing, not a blessed
> thing. People on this reserve are still afraid of them.

RODNEY:
> Who?

ANNE:
> The C.A.S. I was storming their offices in downtown
> Toronto when you were still in diapers, boy. They'd had
> their screaming Indian women before but I took the
> cake. Wouldn't leave—I sat down and said I wasn't going
> to let up till I'd seen my own daughter's file.

RODNEY:
> What happened?

ANNE:
> They called the cops and threw me in their car. Real

rough on me, too! Said I was "fixated." Find me a
mother in my situation who isn't. Them people,
they're no damn good. Cradle snatchers. That's
the whole long and short of it, nothing more than
common kidnappers!

RODNEY:

But Anne, they got Indian case workers now. Hell, my
aunt's been working with them for years.

ANNE:

And I've had my suspicions about your Aunt Julia,
Rodney. No offence.

RODNEY:

Okay, but you take away the C.A.S. and who is gonna
look after the kids who are really getting hurt?

ANNE:

Let our own people tell them who they should take, and
where they should take them, and for how long. Don't
let them come walking in cool as the breeze into our
homes without so much as a knock on the door and do
their dirty work with no one to stop them from stealing
our babies right from our breasts. We got to get in there
now and get them kids back on the reserves.

RODNEY:

Uh, Anne, my aunt once told me about this Cree girl that
was taken out of her community when she was four
years old and raised by white parents.

ANNE:

Thieves!

RODNEY:

And after 10 years in court, her reserve got her
returned.

ANNE:

See, I told you it could be done.

RODNEY:
> Think about it. This teenager, raised in the city, forcibly
> taken from the white family she grew up with and loved,
> shipped off to this isolated reserve way up north, where
> she didn't know anybody, or even the language. She was
> living in poverty for the first time in her life. She didn't
> know how to relate, make friends, how to live. She
> didn't fit in. She was gang raped by a group of boys on
> the reserve. Nobody likes an outsider.

ANNE:
> Where was that girl's mother? Where was her family?
> That story should have been a happy story. That's not
> like me, Rodney. I'd make sure she fit in.

Barb enters from the bathroom.

BARB:
> The first thing I want to do is plug that damn hole in the
> bathroom wall. Talk about freezing your buns off. Mom,
> can I borrow ten thousand?

ANNE:
> Oh, leave me alone.

Barb is looking out the window.

BARB:
> We could put the satellite dish right up over the dog-
> house. Then maybe we could get a dog. Not a reserve
> mongrel, but one of those purebreds, something with
> class. (*her eyes light up and she relishes the words*) A
> pit bull. (*to her mother*) Oh, Mom, bring it out. Can I
> touch it again, huh?

Anne brings out the cheque.

ANNE:
> Until we figure out what to do with it, I'm going to put it
> away in a safe place.

Anne gets up to put the cheque in a jar on a high shelf.

BARB:
But, Mom! What if the house burns down or something?

Anne reconsiders and climbs back down.

ANNE:
I guess we should go see a banker or something tomorrow.

Barb breathes a sigh of relief. As Anne returns she passes the photograph on the wall. It slows her down.

ANNE:
Time to come to my senses, too. I know I'm stubborn but it shouldn't take two dozen detectives to drill it into my skull. Court records are classified. Adoption records are sealed. There's no way of finding out. That was my last hope.

RODNEY:
We put you on the adoption registry.

ANNE:
I know what the chances are of anything happening with that. She probably doesn't even know it exists. I didn't. I wonder if she has a happy life.

BARB:
I'm sure she did, Mom.

Infuriated by the past tense, Anne looks at her daughter with rage, but the emotion slowly burns out. Anne leaves the room. There is a terrible silence.

RODNEY:
So what are you two fun-loving girls planning to do for Christmas?

Barb is still looking off after her mother.

BARB:

Wanna help pick out the tree on Saturday? If you want, you can spend Christmas with us, too. Mom told me to ask you. You can help us do the tree on Christmas Eve.

RODNEY:

(*backing off*) Now Barb . . . that's a family sort of thing.

BARB:

(*bristling*) I take it you don't want to spend Christmas with us?

RODNEY:

I have my own family, Barb.

BARB:

It's not as if your family would miss you for a few hours.

RODNEY:

Ah, I have other plans.

BARB:

I see. Well, maybe you'll find the time to at least visit us on Christmas Day.

RODNEY:

Don't be that way. I've got my reasons.

BARB:

You've got excuses. Every time something comes up that's important to me, you make excuses.

RODNEY:

For instance?

BARB:

The tenth anniversary of my father's passing away. You didn't even bother to show up for the dinner.

RODNEY:

That's not fair. I was . . . busy.

BARB:
> You had a bowling tournament. A bowling tournament is not busy, it's an insult.

RODNEY:
> It was a curling bonspiel, not bowling!

BARB:
> Details.

RODNEY:
> And it was the league finals, too, which goes to show what a great interest you take in what's important to me. It's getting late.

Rodney turns to leave. Barb is disgusted.

BARB:
> You always do that.

RODNEY:
> Do what?

BARB:
> Wimp out in the middle of an argument. It drives me crazy, Rod. You won't even stand there and fight with me like a man.

RODNEY:
> I will argue with you, Barb. But I just don't see the point of fighting about something, getting all emotional over it. It just clouds the issue rather than helping you reach any kind of understanding. And besides, when you start a fight, you always end up doing both parts yourself, anyway. I think I'd better go.

BARB:
> Yeah, you'd better go. See ya.

Rodney opens the door to leave. Barb follows him and looks outside.

BARB:
> (*annoyed*) Great, it's snowing. Looks like it's going to be an even whiter Christmas.

She slams the door behind him.

RODNEY:
> I get the feeling it's sure going to be a cold one.

Rodney moves out into the cold winter night.

RODNEY:
> I know what you're thinking. Shallow, egocentric man afraid of commitment. Oh, shut up. I have my reasons, trust me, and they're good ones. So I don't like Christmas, the once-a-year generosity and syrupy good will, the sappiness. Ever wonder why there are so many diabetics in the world? Even so, I'm tired of being portrayed as Otter Lake's version of The Grinch. I don't want to steal Christmas, I just want to ignore it, but it won't ignore me. (*starts singing*) "You're a mean one, Mr. Rodney." (*he gets agitated*) My shoes aren't too tight. My head is screwed on just right. And my heart isn't two sizes too small. Bah humbug.

He moves off as we hear the sound of a telephone ringing and "All My Children" coming from the television. Anne is watching it and calls off stage.

ANNE:
> Barb, can you get the phone? I'm in the middle of "All My Children." This is where we find out who—

Barb is entering from another room and moves through the kitchen to the telephone.

BARB:
> Spare me. Last time I let you sucker me in I ended up taking a week off work just to find out who the father of somebody's baby is. If I want that stuff I'll visit next door.

She picks up the receiver.

BARB:
> What? . . . Of course it's me, Vanessa. I live here . . .
> Calm down . . . What kind of information? . . . Are you
> kidding? . . . Did she say why? . . . By name? . . . Oh my
> God, yeah okay . . . Let me get a pencil. (*she finds one*)
> Okay, shoot. (*she writes a short message*) Thanks,
> Vanessa.

*She hangs up. There is a timid rapping at the door, and
Rodney slowly peeks his head in.*

RODNEY:
> Snooky pie, I had time to think about last night.

BARB:
> There's a first time for everything.

RODNEY:
> Let me finish. If it's really important to you, I'd be
> delighted to come over and help you decorate the tree.
> Oh gee, sweetums, how do I let you talk me into these
> things, eh? One minute I'm planning to be home safely
> tomorrow night drinking eggnog by the pailful. Well,
> actually, it's my brother's new recipe for eggnog. He
> calls it "beernog." So it looks like I'm all yours instead.

BARB:
> Not now, Rodney.

RODNEY:
> How about this? Let me take you into town tonight and
> I'll buy you dinner. Better grab it cuz after you cash that
> cheque you'll be buying me dinner for the rest of your
> life.

No comment from Barb.

RODNEY:
> How about a movie or a couple of beers? We haven't

been out on the town in a while. Consider it a
congratulatory outing.

BARB:

No, thank you.

RODNEY:

How about a boot to the forehead?

BARB:

(*not listening*) Not tonight.

RODNEY:

What's the matter with you? You look like you've seen a
ghost.

BARB:

Close. Vanessa just called from the band office and she
says, "Barb, I just got the strangest call at the band
office," and I figure, well, that's your job, honey, you
took it, but she tells me this woman was asking for information from her, a certain type of information, and you
know how Vanessa loves to drag things out till you want
to strangle her, but I didn't give her the satisfaction. I
just waited. "Old information," she says, "from over 30
years ago." She says this woman started off real vague,
asking about any kind of information about Indian kids
taken away for adoption during that time. And then she
goes, "Listen to this. She starts getting specific," she
says, "and she mentioned your mother by name." My
mother. It's about Grace.

RODNEY:

Did she leave any number or anything?

BARB:

Yeah, she said to call Janice Wirth at some law office and
gave a phone number in Toronto.

Rodney takes the slip of paper and reads it.

RODNEY:
You'd better tell her.

BARB:
No, you.

RODNEY:
She's your mother.

BARB:
But she likes you better.

RODNEY:
Barb, you have to tell her.

Anne has entered during this last part and hangs back in the doorway.

ANNE:
Tell me what?

BARB:
What if it's a false alarm?

ANNE:
What if what is a false alarm? Who was that on the phone?

RODNEY:
It doesn't matter. She has a right to know.

ANNE:
Somebody around here better tell me something soon.

BARB:
Yesterday she was ready to put all this behind her. Why open a new wound?

ANNE:
It's about my baby, isn't it?

BARB:
> You see? Do you hear that? Do you hear it?! Mom is
> expecting a dependent seven-month-old baby to come
> walking through those doors and into her arms. She'll
> wanna breastfeed this woman. If this is Grace, she will
> be a 35-year-old woman with a set of parents and a full
> history. Mom doesn't want that. And what if she's heard
> about the money? It's possible. We've been in all the
> papers. Don't you find it a bit coincidental that she
> phoned just after we picked up the cheque? I don't
> wanna think it but I have to. What if she's after the
> money, or a cut of it anyways? In your condition, you'd
> give her the whole five million at the drop of a hat. I
> have nothing more to say on the subject. I will not open
> my mouth again. Here's the slip of paper. The name is
> Janice Wirth, she must be representing Grace. That's
> the phone number of a law firm. Bains, Kapelle, and
> David. Dial one first.

*Barb hands her the piece of paper and sits down, facing
away from her mother. Anne stares down at the paper.
Rodney doesn't know where to look. Slowly, Anne moves
towards the phone. She picks up the receiver and dials
with aching slowness. It rings. When she finally hears a
voice on the other end, she passes the phone over to a
surprised Barb.*

ANNE:
> Barb! Barb!

*Barb hesitates, looks at the phone, looks up at God, and then
marches over to the phone. She takes it from her mother. She
freezes on the line, then quickly passes it over to Rodney.*

RODNEY:
> What? Oh, why me?

BARB:
> Just take it.

He moves across the kitchen and takes the phone.

RODNEY:

(*on phone*) Janice Wirth please. (*silence*) I'm phoning
on behalf of the Wabungs . . . No, I'm just a friend of the
family . . . Mrs. Wabung is very anxious to speak with
her daughter . . .

ANNE:

Not on the phone. Tell her not on the phone.

RODNEY:

(*on phone*) I'm sorry, what was that? . . . But wouldn't it
be better if Grace talked personally with the family? . . .
Oh, I see . . . Ah, it's kind of hard to explain. The house
is just up from the band office. Just turn right at the big
pine tree . . . Yes, yes, I'll pass the message along.

Rodney hangs up.

ANNE:

Well, is she going to get the message along to Grace?

RODNEY:

Sort of. Janice Wirth *is* Grace. She'll be here early
tomorrow afternoon.

BARB:

Mom, are you okay?

ANNE:

Tomorrow. That doesn't give us much time.

BARB:

Time for what?

ANNE:

Look at this place. It's a mess. It's a dump. How could I
live like this?

BARB:

Calm down, Mom.

ANNE:
I've got to buy groceries. She'll probably be half-starved
to death. What should I cook? She's probably used to
white food. I sure can't cook her Indian food then. What
do white people eat, Rodney?

RODNEY:
Stuff like whole wheat and yoghurt.

ANNE:
I gotta remember to get some of that stuff. Whole wheat
and yoghurt. Oh, and the tree. The Christmas tree. Will
your brother lend us the car again, do you think? Then we
can be a real family. We can all decorate the tree together
like they do in the movies. Get us a nice tree, Rodney.

*Anne begins hauling things, everything, from cupboards
high and low.*

RODNEY:
Anne, how long have you been on amphetamines?

BARB:
You wanna make a shopping list, Mom, or should I just
bring home the whole store?

ANNE:
I told you my baby would come home someday. She's
coming home! She's coming home!

BARB:
Come on, Rod.

*Anne is cleaning a mile a minute. Barb and Rodney quickly
throw their outdoor gear on.*

RODNEY:
Well, I think we've made her day, wouldn't you say?

BARB:
Perhaps too much.

RODNEY:
> This may turn out to be wonderful. Hell, you may even like Grace. After all these years you'll finally have someone to play Barbie dolls with.

BARB:
> You're such an optimist.

RODNEY:
> I have to be, dating you.

Rodney and Barb exit.

The stage is lit by twinkling snow crystals, transforming the bleak snowbanks into the gateway of a magical winter wonderland. Very subtly, a tinkling music plays within this soft spectacle. The image is "Peace On Earth." We hear the sound of a car engine pulling up in the near distance, then the sound of a Christmas tree being removed from the roofrack of a car. A sluggish Barb and Rodney come schlumping on with an absolutely stunning, if cumbersome, blue spruce Christmas tree.

RODNEY:
> I gotta admit, it's a great tree.

BARB:
> She's already got the place picked out. Over in the corner.

RODNEY:
> Why there? You've never had it there before.

BARB:
> That's where Grace's crib was. In that very corner. She installed the hot water tank where mine used to be. Should we take the tree in now?

RODNEY:
> Naw, why take it in now when you don't need it till tonight? Let's just leave it on the snowbank. It'll keep longer.

They throw the tree on the snowbank.

BARB:
Thank your brother for letting us use his car.

RODNEY:
You got it. In fact, I'll go do that right now. Bye, sweetheart.

Rodney turns to leave but Barb cuts him off.

BARB:
You son of a . . . You're backing out again.

RODNEY:
What backing out?

BARB:
You made a commitment.

RODNEY:
But honey buns . . .

BARB:
I don't want the three of us here alone. It would seem too . . . private, too soon. I need insulation, a buffer. I need you to buff.

RODNEY:
But "How the Grinch Stole Christmas" is on tonight. You know that's the only tolerable thing about this whole holiday mess.

BARB:
Rodney, please.

RODNEY:
I hate it when you do that. All this being included in the family is too close to being married, but I'll stay on one condition—that you'll do the tree decorating without me.

BARB:
Not exactly a pledge of undying love, but I guess it's the most I can expect. You'll stay until eight?

RODNEY:
Six.

BARB:
Seven-thirty.

RODNEY:
Six-thirty.

BARB/RODNEY:
Seven!

BARB:
It's a deal.

Barb happily kisses Rodney, deeply.

RODNEY:
Okay, seven-thirty.

BARB:
I'll even sweeten the pot. Stay for dinner?

Rodney pulls away suspiciously.

RODNEY:
What do I have to cook and how many dishes do I have to wash?

BARB:
Don't be that way. The dinner is free from any and all obligations.

RODNEY:
Said the spider to the fly.

Barb kisses him quickly and runs into the house, turning

just before she enters. She gestures for him to come in. Rodney returns the wave and smiles half-heartedly.

RODNEY:
Lost again.

Rodney runs to join her. Barb and Rodney enter the house as Anne begins shoving a wild rice stuffing up a plucked goose's bum. Anne never stops working as she talks.

BARB:
It smells like a forest in here.

ANNE:
That's the Pine Sol. Out of my way or I'll stuff you, too.

Rodney and Barb move to the side.

BARB:
Sorry.

ANNE:
Barb, put the good tablecloth on for me, will you?

Barb complies.

ANNE:
Well, did you get it?

RODNEY:
Got you the best damn . . . darned tree in the province. Once Grace sees that tree, she'll be so overcome by the spirit of Christmas she'll never leave, and you'll all live so happily ever after.

ANNE:
Thank you, Rodney, but that's a little thick.

BARB:
Haa!

RODNEY:
> Fine, but it's still a nice tree. You got anything to drink, Anne?

ANNE:
> I believe Barb picked up some pop this morning with the groceries.

Barb climbs down from cleaning the clock.

BARB:
> Yeah, in the fridge. Get me one, too, will you? Bottom shelf of the door, left side. By the yoghurt.

Rodney pulls out two soft drinks.

ANNE:
> Barb, open the oven.

Anne puts the bird in the roasting pan.

ANNE:
> I wish Frank were here to see this.

RODNEY:
> It is a nice bird.

BARB:
> She means Grace.

RODNEY:
> Oh.

The goose fits snugly in the oven, hidden from further scrutiny to do its cooking.

ANNE:
> Nothing like a good goose at Christmas time, that's for sure.

Rodney moves forward to either act on or say something in

response to such a good straight line, but Barb cuts him off with a warning.

BARB:
> (*to Rodney*) Don't even think it! (*to Anne*) Well, that's sure the biggest goose I've seen today.

RODNEY:
> (*to Barb*) Killjoy. (*to Anne*) What kind of fixings have you got to go with that thing?

ANNE:
> Mashed potatoes, carrots, bannock, my gravy, and to top it all off, my famous grapefruit pie.

Barb notices the table stacked with dinner utensils.

BARB:
> The good dishes, too.

ANNE:
> Yep.

BARB:
> Real napkins instead of paper towels?

ANNE:
> Naturally.

BARB:
> Aw, darn! And my party dress is still at the cleaners.

ANNE:
> Not any more. I picked it up this morning after I finished my shopping. It's on your bed.

BARB:
> You're gonna make me get all dressed up for this?

ANNE:
> I'm not going to make you do anything, Barbara Louella.

BARB:

Aha! Resorting to middle names, are we? Don't threaten me, Mom. Suppose I refuse to get dressed up?

ANNE:

Then that's your decision.

BARB:

That's it?

ANNE:

If you want your sister to see the way you dress, then that's your business.

BARB:

If she's my sister then she'll just have to accept me the way I am.

ANNE:

Don't pout.

BARB:

I'm not pouting.

ANNE:

You're pouting.

BARB:

So what if I am? Look at all this! I never got this, not when I graduated high school, not even when I saved that kid from drowning. And I hate grape-fruit pie!

She storms off to her room.

ANNE:

Sometimes I wonder if she put me through those 30 hours of labour on purpose.

Rodney looks down at himself.

RODNEY:
 Nobody told me this was semiformal.

Barb storms back in, toothbrush in her mouth, paste and foam dribbling down her chin, swipes her purse off the back of a kitchen chair, and marches off to the bathroom. She mumbles and grumbles incoherently throughout. Anne removes her apron and hangs it up. For the first time, we really see her brand-spanking new dress, and it's lovely.

RODNEY:
 Wow! Nice dress, Anne. Or should I say Elizabeth Taylor?

ANNE:
 Oh, go on.

RODNEY:
 Oh, sorry.

ANNE:
 No, I meant, go on!

RODNEY:
 May I have this dance?

Anne giggles and pushes him away.

ANNE:
 You're crazy. I'm an old woman.

RODNEY:
 Not in that dress you aren't.

Rodney takes her into his arms and they begin a gentle two-step around the kitchen to the country Christmas music that is now playing on the radio. The two-step should become fairly expert, and fun to watch, peppered with Anne's laughter and efforts to match her partner. Finally the song ends.

RODNEY:
 (*bowing*) Thank you for that delightful dance.

ANNE:
You're welcome, fine sir. (*she wipes her forehead*) Oh
my, I'm getting old. I haven't danced like that with a
man since Frank.

RODNEY:
I'm honoured.

ANNE:
You should be. I was 16 the first time he spoke to me.
He was 19 and so worldly. He'd lived in town for a
whole year. Mom and Dad didn't like him much. His
English was too good, they said. One day he asked me,
"Anne, will you come out with me to see a movie?" Oh,
nobody in the village went to see movies, but Frank
wanted me to go with him. We had a hard time
convincing my parents to let me go. I know this
sounds horrible, but Frank sort of bought me.

RODNEY:
Bought you?

ANNE:
He offered my father 30 pickerel to let me go to the
movies with him. Today it sounds bad but at least we
got out.

*Barb emerges one more time to get a towel from the bath-
room. She is half-dressed and still fuming.*

BARB:
I don't need this, Mother. I could be out having fun, but
no. I'll put up with this even though every fibre of my
body is rebelling. I just thought you should know.

*She disappears behind a slammed door. Anne and Rodney
carry on as though nothing has happened.*

ANNE:
Well, Friday came and he arrived in his pickup truck
with different coloured doors on it. In town there was a

whole line-up of white people right around the corner.
Some of them looked at us funny. I just looked down.
I still have trouble looking white people in the eye.
But not Frank. He looked right back. They didn't look
much longer. And the smell inside that place, reeking
of popcorn and butter. So messy that place, and dirty.
Torn tickets, spilled popcorn, paper cups and gum
wrappers, everything. I was embarrassed for the people.
But those big red comfortable seats . . . I could have
slept there.

RODNEY:
> What was the movie?

ANNE:
> It was called *Rear Window*. It took me a while to get
> into it. You gotta understand, I'd never seen a movie
> before, or even been in an apartment building. So it took
> me a while, but pretty soon I got to like it. I even found
> it funny. Reminded me of home, those people looking
> out their windows at other people's business. I loved it.
> From then on, we practically lived in that theatre. We
> were married a year later and spent our wedding night
> there.

RODNEY:
> Your wedding night?

ANNE:
> It was a double feature.

RODNEY:
> In a strange sort of way, it's kind of romantic.

*Barb comes in furiously, wearing a dress more appropriate
for a New Year's dance, and holds out her arms.*

BARB:
> How's this? Happy?

She plunks herself miserably on a kitchen chair.

RODNEY:
> Barb, you look so . . . feminine.

Barb's arms swing in circles towards herself, welcoming more abuse.

BARB:
> Okay, come on. Let's get it over with, the shots.

ANNE:
> Now, Barb, you look just fine. Grace will be proud to have you for a sister.

BARB:
> Grace. Well, I gotta admit, I'm curious. I wonder what she'll look like?

ANNE:
> Well, she was bigger than you as a baby. More hair, too. She used to laugh so much, hardly ever cried. That baby, just a mother's dream. Your brother favoured your father. I always thought Grace took after me.

BARB:
> Will you quit making her into this fantastic mythic person? You don't know anything about her and you're building her up to be this perfect woman. I could never live up to your image of St. Grace of the Perpetual Memory. How do you expect her to? She's not Christ returning from the desert!

Anne draws in her breath quickly and rises from the table, her eyes aflame at the sacrilege. Suddenly, the sound of a car approaching can be heard. The action freezes for a moment, and they all listen.

ANNE:
> Oh my God, is it . . . ?

BARB:
> Rodney, check it out.

Rodney takes a look out the window, craning his neck to see down the road.

RODNEY:
It's a car.

BARB:
We know that.

RODNEY:
It's a nice car. One of those fancy expensive ones. A Saab, I think.

ANNE:
Can you see her? Can you see her?

RODNEY:
Not yet. Too much glare.

ANNE:
I can't look. I can't look. Let me know when you can see her.

RODNEY:
She may have been born here but she sure doesn't know a damn thing about country roads. She's skidding all over the place.

Anne rises again in alarm.

BARB:
Take it easy, Mom.

RODNEY:
Look out! Look out!

ANNE/BARB:
What?! What?!

RODNEY:
She just said hello to the snowdrift. She's really in there.

ANNE:
> Is she okay?

RODNEY:
> I can't tell. Wait a minute. The door's opening.

BARB:
> Yeah, and . . .

RODNEY:
> Wow.

BARB:
> What the hell does "wow" mean?

ANNE:
> Watch your tongue.

RODNEY:
> It means . . . "wow."

BARB:
> Could you be a little more specific?

RODNEY:
> It means she's impressive.

BARB:
> (*yelling*) What does "impressive" mean? Oh, get out of the way!

Barb rushes to the window, pushing Rodney aside, and looks out.

BARB:
> (*disgusted*) Impressive. (*she looks and looks*) I don't see her. Where is she?

Rodney runs back to the window.

RODNEY:
> She was there a moment ago.

BARB:
> Car looks kind of flashy.

RODNEY:
> Where'd she go?

ANNE:
> Is she all right?

BARB:
> I don't know. She seems to have disappeared.

ANNE:
> Not again.

RODNEY:
> She must be out there somewhere. I'd better go take a look.

He starts getting his outdoor clothes on.

ANNE:
> Please, let her be okay. Barb, you'd better go with him.

BARB:
> Mom, look at me!

ANNE:
> Barb!!

Barb reluctantly starts putting on her outdoor clothes and her down parka.

RODNEY:
> Let's go!

BARB:
> Well, give me a second.

Anne, who has run off, quickly reenters with a blanket.

ANNE:
Have you found her yet?

RODNEY:
On our way.

ANNE:
Rodney, take this with you.

Barb, fancy party dress, mukluks, parka, and toque is now ready.

BARB:
Okay, let's go find the chick.

Barb opens the door to find the radiant Grace standing there in a magnificent white fur coat, hat, and muff. The sun just happens to be at her back, giving her the kind of backlighting you can't pay people for. Anne gasps slightly, Rodney smiles appreciatively, and Barb, stunned, says,

BARB:
Wow.

The lights fade out.

END OF ACT ONE

Act II

It is a few minutes later. An overhead spotlight tightly frames the fabulous white fur coat, carelessly thrown over a kitchen chair. The silhouettes of Anne, Barb, and Rodney are seen, each standing alone in this uncomfortable kitchen. Barb's hand is reaching towards the coat. The action is frozen except for Rodney.

RODNEY:

Well, she's here. Grace the memory has become Grace the woman. And what a woman. She may be everything Barb feared and everything Anne hoped for. Not a good mixture for the likes of this family. Look at Barb reaching for that coat. Anne hasn't said a word since Grace got here five minutes ago. And here I am in the middle of this whole incredible spectacular reunion. It just goes to prove how stupid I am.

Barb's hand moves towards the coat and as it reaches into the light, we hear the loud enthusiastic flushing of a toilet, and the 60-watt reality of the kitchen is restored. Barb backs away from the coat, like a child caught doing something naughty. She looks at her mother, who is staring off towards the bathroom, lost in a million thoughts. Water runs in the bathroom sink. Barb takes a step towards Rodney, and their eyes meet. He looks at Anne, then towards the bathroom. Barb approaches the coat again and touches it, letting her palms run over the soft, beautiful fur. The running water has stopped. Barb picks up the fur coat as Janice enters from the bathroom, drying her hands. Barb looks like a fox caught with a rabbit in its mouth. She freezes. Janice looks at her carefully, then smiles.

JANICE:
> Would you like to try it on?

Anne, a bundle of nervous energy, quickly tries to finish tidying up. She grabs Barb's and Rodney's jackets, folded over a chair, and hangs them up neatly. She also moves a few more coats to make room on a peg for Janice's large fur coat.

BARB:
> Me? No.

JANICE:
> It would probably fit you.

BARB:
> (*nervously*) No, no. I was just going to hang it up. We needed the extra chair and half of it was on the floor, and it's such a beautiful coat I didn't want it to get dirty.

Barb quickly tries to change the subject as she gives Anne the coat to hang up.

BARB:
> How was the bathroom?

Barb winces at her stupid and nervous question.

JANICE:
> Brisk.

BARB:
> You mean cold. Yeah, we've been meaning to have that hole repaired, but we never seem to get around to it or have the money. You get used to it after a while. The cold, I mean. It's been about twelve years for us. Having the hole. In the wall in the bathroom. Ever since Dad almost shot Mom.

Janice reacts with shock.

BARB:
> I mean he didn't know she was on the toilet. He was outside cleaning his gun and saw this big rabbit by the house. Dad was about to shoot it when Nemush, that was our dog, came racing for it. The rabbit. Dad jerked the shotgun and hit the house. I mean he wouldn't ordinarily take a shotgun to a rabbit, but that's what he was cleaning at the time. Would have had strips of rabbit. Rabbit fingers. Anyway, the point is he nearly bagged Mom. Boy, did she scream. Damn near took her foot off. Mom was real mad.

Anne looks up briefly, then lowers her eyes.

BARB:
> That's how the hole got there.

JANICE:
> Quite a story.

BARB:
> Quite a hole.

Rodney gently taps Janice on the shoulder. She turns and studies him intently.

RODNEY:
> Um, excuse me . . .

JANICE:
> You're not my . . .

RODNEY:
> No, no, just a friend. Rodney, the voice on the phone? Um, I thought you might want to know, your shoes are bleeding.

Janice looks at him, confused, then looks down at her red shoes, which are dripping red water.

ANNE:
> Oh my goodness!

JANICE:
I can't believe it—they're Italian leather and the dye is running!

RODNEY:
Haemorrhaging is more like it.

JANICE:
I hope they won't stain your floor. They won't, will they? Oh I'm so sorry. Look at your floor.

Janice takes them off and turns around quickly, accidentally bumping Rodney with the shoes, leaving a red stain on his shirt. Rodney's hands instinctively come up to grab the shoes. Janice is horrified at what she's done and covers her mouth with her hand in shock.

JANICE:
Oh, I'm sorry.

She takes her hand away, leaving a red hand print on her face.

JANICE:
Let me clean that up.

She grabs a dishtowel from the table to wipe off Rodney's stain. Instead she succeeds in knocking the plate of bannock it was draped over, onto the chair. Reacting in surprise, Janice then knocks over the chair and it lands on Barb's foot. Bannock goes flying like buckshot and Rodney dodges it as Barb hops around holding her injured foot.

JANICE:
Shit.

Barb and Rodney instantly look towards Anne who politely pretends not to hear. The once magnificent Janice is now like the rest of them.

RODNEY:
You really are related to Barb.

JANICE:
I don't believe this is happening to me.

RODNEY:
I look like I've been shot, and we've been bombed by bannock.

ANNE:
Are you okay?

Barb nurses her bruised foot.

BARB:
Is *she* okay?

Anne tries to wipe the stain off Rodney's belly. Janice and Barb bend down to pick up the bannock and bump their heads. They nervously smile at each other as they gather bread together. Rodney, a red shoe in each hand, bangs them together three times.

RODNEY:
"There's no place like home, there's no place like home . . . "

ANNE:
(*in Ojibway*) Stop it, Rodney!

Chastised, Rodney puts the shoes down and dries his hands of the dye.

ANNE:
Grace, you sit down, and I'll get you something to wear.

Anne exits to get a pair of moccasins.

BARB:
Uh, you've got some dye on your face.

Janice, cringing in embarrassment, checks out her reflection in the nearest available shiny surface.

JANICE:
I don't believe this. You must all think I'm a complete idiot.

She walks back, having wiped most of the dye off. A little dab remains below her ear, hidden by her hair.

RODNEY:
(*still fiddling with his shirt*) Not a complete one. So how was the drive up?

JANICE:
Apart from that vicious snowbank out front? Uneventful, except I missed the turnoff. I'm not used to these small side roads. I found myself driving on this bumpy road through a very large field. I pulled over to ask this gentleman for directions. He told me to be quiet. I asked why. "Because I'm fishing" he said.

RODNEY:
It's a little early to be driving across Chemong Lake.

BARB:
You could have been drowned!

JANICE:
Drowned? I was driving on water?!

RODNEY:
You got guts, lady.

JANICE:
But the road . . .

BARB:
. . . turns into a snowmobile trail.

JANICE:
So that's why that man kept moving away from me and my car.

RODNEY:
Strange guy, walked with a limp, very thick glasses, seemed to be having a conversation with himself?

JANICE:
Yes, that's him. Is he the local eccentric?

Anne reenters the room.

RODNEY:
Sort of.

BARB:
He's also your cousin.

JANICE:
Perfect.

ANNE:
(*she hands Janice the moccasins*) Try these on.

JANICE:
Oh, they're beautiful. Look at that workmanship. Do these designs mean anything? Or perhaps the colours?

Barb decides to have some fun. She talks very seriously.

BARB:
Oh yes, they do. They refer to the four colours of man.

JANICE:
But aren't there five colours?

BARB:
Five colours? (*Barb thinks fast*) Oh, that's because the fifth colour represents the mixing of the races and . . .

ANNE:
Barb!

BARB:
   Aw, Mom.

ANNE:
   They're just flowers.

JANICE:
   The smell is unusual.

ANNE:
   That's from the tanning and smoking.

JANICE:
   You smoke leather, like ham?

BARB:
   Yeah, but ham's harder to wear.

Anne gives her a "shut-your-face" glare.

BARB:
   (*sighs*) Yes, Mother.

Janice puts the moccasins on.

JANICE:
   They fit.

BARB:
   Mom makes them.

JANICE:
   Your work is beautiful. This may sound . . . Oh, this is
   awkward. I'm afraid I'm not sure what I should call you.
   Mrs. Wabung? Anne?

ANNE:
   Whatever you feel comfortable with.

BARB:
   What about "Mom"?

Janice smiles, embarrassed. Anne gives Barb a stern look that wilts Barb.

ANNE:
> (*in Ojibway*) Don't push her. Stay out of this!

BARB:
> Yeah, okay. Hey, Rodney, let's go take care of that stain before it sets in. You two just . . . whatever.

Barb ushers Rodney off to a bedroom. There is a silence as both Anne and Janice struggle for something to say. Barb walks to the bathroom carrying Rodney's stained shirt.

RODNEY:
> (*off stage*) But I'm cold.

BARB:
> Just sit there and don't move.

Rodney's voice can be heard off stage.

RODNEY:
> That's how I talk to my dog.

Barb notices Janice and Anne watching her.

BARB:
> I'll be doing this in there. Bye.

Barb disappears into the bathroom. Anne notices the smudge of red under Janice's ear.

ANNE:
> You've still got some red on your face.

JANICE:
> I thought I got it all. Where is it?

ANNE:
> Here.

Anne grabs a cloth and moves towards Janice. She cups the opposite side of Janice's head with her hand, wets a small part of the cloth with her tongue, and wipes her face as if she were a child. The closeness to her long lost child begins to affect her. Her voice quivers, her heart is beating a mile a minute. Even though the job is all finished, she doesn't remove her hand. They stare into each other's eyes, and Anne slowly pulls Janice closer until they are hugging.

ANNE:
Grace . . .

Anne pulls back slightly, tears in her eyes, and a little embarrassed. Too much too soon.

ANNE:
So many questions for you. Thirty-five years of questions.

JANICE:
Me, too.

The millions of questions go through each of their minds, each trying to figure out the appropriate first one.

ANNE:
Where did you grow up?

JANICE:
In southern Ontario, London actually.

ANNE:
I've been there. Oh my, I could have passed you on the street. The people that raised you, what were they like?

JANICE:
They took me around the world.

ANNE:
Brothers? Sisters?

JANICE:

Two brothers.

ANNE:

Where were you in the family?

JANICE:

They are both older. Gregory's in Germany right now
and Marshall lives in Vancouver.

ANNE:

Really, so far apart. Most of our family still live around
here. Marshall and Gregory, huh? What was that other
name you go by?

JANICE:

Janice.

ANNE:

That's a pretty name.

JANICE:

Thank you. I was named after my mother's grandmother.
She was a—

ANNE:

You were named after Grace Kelly.

JANICE:

I beg your pardon?

ANNE:

Grace Kelly. You were named after Grace Kelly.

JANICE:

I was?

ANNE:

Rear Window was the first movie me and your father
ever saw. You were born the year *High Society* came
out. You were named after Grace Kelly.

JANICE:

Grace Kelly. Interesting.

ANNE:

I think she was one of the most elegant ladies I ever saw. I wanted my daughter to grow up just like her. Tall, beautiful, can look life in the face. And look. Look at you, Grace.

JANICE:

You've never seen me in the morning. I like her, too. What's your favourite movie of hers?

ANNE:

Oh *High Noon* for sure. I thought she was simply marvellous in it, just waiting around for Gary Cooper to get killed. Marvellous. Westerns have always been my favourites.

JANICE:

Even the ones where the Indians get killed?

ANNE:

Well, they weren't real Indians. What kind of movie do you like? Have you ever seen *The Magnificent Seven* with that bald-headed guy, what's-his-name?

JANICE:

Yul Brynner.

ANNE:

Yes, Yul Brynner.

JANICE:

A long time ago. But I prefer the original, Akira Kurosawa's *The Seven Samurai*. You know, with Toshiro Mifune. I find it a better, more complex film.

ANNE:

What year was it made?

JANICE:
Fifty-four. Why?

ANNE:
Must have missed that one in Peterborough. Maybe me and Barb will rent it sometime, *The Seven Salmon Eyes?*

JANICE:
(*smiling*) Samurai.

ANNE:
Samurai.

JANICE:
It's one of my mother's . . . favourite films. She had actually studied in Japan for a number of years just after the war.

ANNE:
She sounds like . . . an interesting woman.

JANICE:
Oh, she is. I owe her a lot.

ANNE:
I'd like to meet her.

Janice looks at her, surprised.

JANICE:
You would?

ANNE:
She's looked after my little girl all these years. Oh yes, I'd like to meet her. Oh, Grace, I gotta know. Are you married? Am I a grandmother?

JANICE:
Sorry, no children, though I haven't quite ruled them out. I was married for two years but that was a long time ago. Too much business, not enough breakfasts for Eric.

He decided to go off and cook for himself.

ANNE:
He didn't like your cooking?

JANICE:
Not much time for cooking. Work keeps me busy.

ANNE:
A lawyer. My daughter the lawyer. Whatever made you become a lawyer?

JANICE:
It's a tradition in the Wirth family.

ANNE:
Do you enjoy it?

JANICE:
That was hardly an issue. Doing well was. It seems in the world of the white middle class, Indians have a reputation for doing things half-assed.

ANNE:
Some people do think like that, don't they? But there's nothing you can do about people like that.

JANICE:
Oh yes, there is. Don't give them anything to be critical of. Be the best. Be untouchable. That's how you get ahead in this life. Even in private school, I tried for valedictorian, the best of the best. That June I wanted to be up there, on the stage, under the awning, while the other girls sat on the lawn getting sunburned.

ANNE:
And did you?

JANICE:
Came in second, and sunburned.

ANNE:
Second is good.

JANICE:
That's what my father said. But it wasn't good enough for me. If I'm in the system, I want to be in the system to win.

ANNE:
You sound like someone from "Dallas" or "Dynasty."

JANICE:
Yes, well, that's my life.

ANNE:
You sound so lonely. I guess it must have been difficult for you. Was school hard on you?

JANICE:
In some ways, not in others. On the volleyball team we were given nicknames to be put on our jackets. I was Pocahontas. At the time I thought it was funny. I always knew I was Indian, but it never actually meant anything to me. Just a fact of life, like being five foot seven. Then Meech Lake happened with Elijah Harper. And Oka. Suddenly everybody was asking me my opinion on this or that situation. They wanted the "Native perspective." But the only perspective I had was a suburban one. I started to wonder about my past, and the more questions I was asked, the more I had questions about myself. Finally, I had to know. I went to London, found the court I was processed in, got my adoption papers, contacted the Department of Indian Affairs, and they eventually told me what reserve I was from. I've had the information for a while. I was too . . . I guess frightened to call, then I saw your pictures in the paper about the lottery. Congratulations by the way. Once I saw your faces, I knew I had to call. To meet you. And here I am. That's my life in a nutshell.

Barb enters the kitchen.

BARB:

That's some nutshell. I was born, went to school in Lakefield, two years of business admin in Peterborough, got my first car at 20, lost my first car at 21. Maybe we better start talking about getting your car out of the snowbank.

JANICE:

Oh, my car! Is there a tow service or something? Someone I can call?

BARB:

As a matter of fact there is. Oh, Rodney darling.

Rodney enters.

RODNEY:

You rang, essence of my existence?

BARB:

(*sweettalking*) I was wondering if you'd like to do your favourite little Barb—

RODNEY:

Little?

Barb quickly tosses him his newly cleaned shirt.

BARB:

There's a car in the drift out there. Make yourself useful. Dig it out. Now.

RODNEY:

But—

BARB:

(*almost yelling*) Now!

RODNEY:

Okay, okay, no problem. I was looking for an exc— I mean something to do.

Rodney puts on his winter stuff.

BARB:
> He's so convenient.

RODNEY:
> Keys, please.

Janice digs them out of the pocket of her coat.

ANNE:
> Do you want to take your tea with you?

RODNEY:
> If I have any more tea, I'll end up in a teatox centre. (*he howls*)

BARB:
> Go!

Rodney opens the door and exits quickly. Anne pours Janice another cup of tea.

ANNE:
> Oh, Grace, I have such wonderful things to show you. Just you sit there and drink your tea.

Anne exits the room.

Rodney is standing outside on the step of the house.

RODNEY:
> As another great man once said, "Free at last, free at last, thank God I'm free at last!" But first Rodney Skywalker and his light shovel must do battle with the evil snow-drift empire.

He handles the shovel like a sword. Rodney, with a bit of a skip to his walk, heads off to do battle with the drift. Barb has taken her teacup and moved to the window to watch Rodney, and Janice follows.

JANICE:
So he belongs to you, huh?

BARB:
Not till he gets his shots. What a nut. He's playing Star Wars again.

JANICE:
How old is he?

BARB:
Chronologically? Twenty-five.

JANICE:
He's cute.

BARB:
So's a puppy.

Janice is amused. Barb plays with her teacup. There is an awkward silence.

JANICE:
Nice dress.

BARB:
Got it last year for New Year's. Yours is pretty, too.

JANICE:
Thank you.

BARB:
Silk, huh? Mine is, too, but it doesn't look like yours for some reason. Oh well, as Rodney says, it's all worm shit anyway.

Barb looks embarrassed but Janice laughs.

JANICE:
I guess.

BARB:
> It goes wonderfully with your coat.

Janice gets up and walks towards her coat.

JANICE:
> Come here.

BARB:
> Huh?

JANICE:
> I want to see how you'd look in my coat.

Barb is surprised.

BARB:
> Your coat?

Janice holds her open coat out, beckoning Barb.

JANICE:
> It won't bite. Try it.

Barb hesitantly gets up and with Janice's help tries the coat on. It feels and looks great on her. She revels in the moment. Janice admires.

JANICE:
> You look wonderful.

BARB:
> I feel wonderful. Can you imagine me walking into the band office with this on? Everybody would be so green with envy, they'd look like martians.

JANICE:
> You should get one. You have the money now.

Barb thinks about it for a moment, then takes the coat off.

BARB:

Oh, I don't think so. Rod and I do a lot of spontaneous things, like snowball fights and stuff. Couldn't do things like that with this kind of jacket. Besides, people don't wear things like this on the reserve unless they catch the animals themselves. It's a little too flashy.

Barb hangs it back up on the peg.

BARB:

You have such a different life. It's like you have every-thing everybody on this reserve doesn't.

JANICE:

Well, I must confess, I did come hoping to impress.

BARB:

Well, you succeeded.

JANICE:

Perhaps too much?

BARB:

You're visiting people with a hole in their bathroom remember? You're something, boy.

JANICE:

How do you mean?

BARB:

Well. Okay, I gotta be honest. When you first called us, I had my apprehensions. The thing that tugged on the hair of my neck was you phoning the day after Mom and I got our lottery cheque. When you walked in that door, after getting out of that fancy car, wearing that beautiful coat of yours, part of me relaxed. I thought, She obviously don't need the money. She has enough of her own. But then another thought kept squirming around inside. Dad always said, "You can use fish to catch fish." You get my meaning? You have to use money to attract money. So there again, I was back in the same position.

JANICE:
And now? What do you think of me now?

BARB:
I'll let you know.

JANICE:
What do you plan to do with all that money?

BARB:
We don't know yet. Spend it, I hope.

JANICE:
Well, whatever you think of me, keep in mind there are people a lot slicker than I am out there. Money like that is a big responsibility.

BARB:
We'll survive.

Anne, a huge smile on her face, enters, her faith in her two daughters solid.

ANNE:
Here, Grace, I've got something to show you. You'll just love it.

Anne puts the albums down on the table with a thump.

JANICE:
Pictures?

ANNE:
Altogether you have 14 aunts and uncles, and too many cousins to count.

JANICE:
And they're all in there?

BARB:
Are you kidding? We have boxes under every bed and in

every closet. Decades of family life and people that
nobody ever looks at.

*Anne opens up one of the multitude of books and starts leaf-
ing through it.*

ANNE:
I look at them. Oh, look, this is your Aunt Erma. Her
place is just four houses down. You must have passed it
on the way. And over here is your cousin John and
cousin Angela. They just got married last year.

JANICE:
Cousins!

BARB:
Relax. Different sides of the family. It gets confusing.

*Anne is so busy and caught up in her adventure that she
really isn't paying attention to what's being said. She
continues pointing at photographs.*

ANNE:
Oh, and look, the wedding reception. There's Uncle
Leon, Buddy, and Michelle. And that's Gertrude. There's
my favourite sister, Esther. I think you've got her nose.

JANICE:
Yes, but she has three of my chins.

ANNE:
There's James. Oh, you've got to meet Shelley. She's so
funny. Janet, Heather, Donna, there's my nephew Bill.

JANICE:
Where does it stop?

BARB:
About next Tuesday.

Janice looks closely at one picture.

JANICE:
You missed him.

ANNE:
(*less enthusiastic*) Oh, that's Duanne. We don't like him.
Remember that.

Janice, confused, turns towards Barb.

BARB:
I'll tell you later.

ANNE:
There's Eunice and her bunch. They live in Ottawa.
That's Becky. She lives in Winnipeg. Michael works
in Kingston. And Johnny is going to see if he can get
a day parole. I'm bringing the whole bunch home for
Christmas.

JANICE:
That should be a very special Christmas.

Anne looks at her daughter lovingly.

ANNE:
A very special one indeed. Now this album I like to call
my Christmas album. I keep all the special pictures of
this merry season in here. Look, here's Barb dressed up
like Santa Claus.

BARB:
Aw, Mom . . .

ANNE:
And there's Barb as an elf.

BARB:
Mom!

ANNE:
Shh, dear. There's Barb as a reindeer.

Janice points to a particular picture that has caught her interest.

JANICE:
He's cute. Who is he?

The smile and enthusiasm drains from Anne. Barb looks uncomfortable.

JANICE:
I'm sorry. Did I say something wrong?

Anne goes for tea.

BARB:
That's Paul.

JANICE:
Paul?

BARB:
Paul. My . . . our brother.

Janice is stunned. She looks at Barb to make sure she's not teasing her again, then studies the picture closely.

BARB:
He died five years ago. A stupid car accident.

Anne is silent by the teapot.

JANICE:
He looks like me. I've never known anyone who looked like me.

Anne, upset, leaves the room in tears. Janice looks worried. Barb has seen this before and is a little concerned.

BARB:
Don't worry, she gets this way, especially on his birthday or the anniversary of his death.

JANICE:

The anniversary . . . ?

BARB:

Yeah. Paul and Rodney were best friends, I mean the
best. One night Rodney phoned from a bar in Lakefield.
He was too drunk to drive. He asked Paul to pick him up
and bring him home. Paul was pissed off but agreed.
About that same time, this other guy, at that same bar,
thought he could drive home. Rodney even saw this guy
leave. Just past the turnoff, this guy hit Paul, head on.
Rodney had to identify the body, and phone Mom.

JANICE:

Oh, God . . .

BARB:

Well, you can figure out how Mom took it. Rodney
disappeared into the city. Since he came back, he started
spending a lot of time around here, with Mom. Maybe he
blames himself. I don't know. He won't talk about it.

JANICE:

What was Paul like?

BARB:

A big lovable goof, Paul was. You would have loved him.
You really would have.

JANICE:

I'm mourning a person I didn't even know.

BARB:

Oh, you knew him. You look like him. When you walked
in that door, I'm sure Mom's heart stopped. Mine almost
did. And you have his drive, that's for sure. Except with
him it was sports. Had to be the best hockey and base-
ball player in the village. It scares me in a way, the
similarities.

Janice closes the book and sits back, solemn.

JANICE:
> Is he buried near here?

BARB:
> About half a mile down the road.

Janice looks towards Anne's bedroom, a worried expression on her face.

JANICE:
> What about Anne?

BARB:
> In a moment she'll come out and try to change the subject. Just go along with her. It makes things easier.

JANICE:
> I wasn't expecting this.

BARB:
> Neither were we.

As if on cue Anne enters, smoothing out her dress.

ANNE:
> Oh my, I'm sorry. I'd forgotten to turn off the iron in my room.

BARB:
> I was just telling Janice about our little house. How old is it, Mom? Almost a hundred years old, eh? Can you believe it? My great-grandfather built it. Do you like it?

Barb urges Janice on.

JANICE:
> Oh yes, it reminds me of our summer cottage a bit.

BARB:
> Really? How?

JANICE:

Both take a hell of a long time to get to. Both are by a lake, and both feel wonderfully homey. We love it there. But I don't get up much any more.

Janice takes her prompting from Barb.

JANICE:

How long have you lived here?

BARB:

Mom's been here all her life. Altogether, about five generations of our family have lived within these walls.

JANICE:

I felt a strong sense of family the moment I stepped in. The place smells of home.

ANNE:

Smells? My place smells?

JANICE:

No, no, no. I didn't mean it like that.

ANNE:

Maybe it's the goose. Could be the Pine Sol.

BARB:

Mom's very thin-skinned about her home. It's very personal to her.

Janice wanders around the kitchen.

JANICE:

As well it should be. A home can tell so much about the people in it. And it's not so much the big things you can get in any department store. I always like knowing about the little things, the everyday things, investigating the nooks and crannies of a place. They're what make a house a home. Like these marks on the wall. I bet there's a story there.

Barb looks nervously at her mother.

BARB:
　　Not really.

JANICE:
　　Oh.

ANNE:
　　Go ahead. Tell her. I'll be all right.

Keeping an eye on Anne, making sure she'll be okay, Barb joins Janice by the marks.

BARB:
　　You sure, Mom? (*Anne nods*) Those lines are a record of me and Paul growing up. Ever since we could stand, Mom would stand us up on our birthdays, and mark our height. The blue marks are Paul, the pink ones are me. If you look closely you can see the dates.

Anne nods. Janice bends over and examines them carefully.

JANICE:
　　Paul kept growing till he was 18. That's old.

BARB:
　　Yeah.

Janice places her back against the wall and measures herself, comparing her height to the marks on the wall.

JANICE:
　　How about that? Just four inches shorter than him.
　　I should be on this wall.

ANNE:
　　You weren't old enough to stand. Paul could stand at 10 months, Barb at 11.

JANICE:
(*almost to herself*) It's not fair.

BARB:
Who said life was fair?

JANICE:
Do you have any more pictures of him?
Any at all?

Anne points to the wall of pictures.

ANNE:
Up there, on the end.

Janice goes to the picture and stares intently at it.

JANICE:
God, he looks so much like me. And these other
pictures?

Janice moves over to look at the other pictures.

ANNE:
Other family.

JANICE:
Some of them are very old.

ANNE:
Some. The one on the right is my grandparents.

JANICE:
Grandparents . . . And this? Who's this chubby little
thing sitting on the big fellow's knee?

ANNE:
It's you. And the man is your father, my Frank.

Janice's breathing is suddenly uneven. She makes an effort to breathe steadily, as if a long even breath will calm her emotions.

JANICE:
My father . . . Dad. (Anne nods) That's what he looked like. He was . . . um . . . very handsome.

ANNE:
Yes, I know.

JANICE:
It said in the article in the paper that you were widowed. Meeting the two of you was all I could think of, I barely thought about . . . Look at his eyes! I'd like a copy of it if I may, and the other one.

ANNE:
They're the only ones I got.

JANICE:
I'll have them copied. He looks so happy. Trustworthy. And there I am on his knee. His hands look so big on me. *(she takes an unsteady sip of her tea)* What did he do to make them take me away?

Barb and Anne look at each other, confused.

ANNE:
What do you mean?

JANICE:
Well, obviously I was taken away for some specific reason. Was it alcohol? I'm sorry for asking so bluntly but you don't grow up a duck in a flock of geese and not wonder why. If it's not too much trouble, I wouldn't mind knowing why.

There is an uncomfortable silence.

ANNE:
It will only make you angry.

JANICE:

I've been angry for almost 35 years. This might stop the anger.

ANNE:

My poor child.

JANICE:

My mother used to say that. I need to know, Anne. I need—somewhere inside—I really need to know why I was put up for adoption. I'm an adult. Please give me the truth.

ANNE:

Cuz we were Indians. Things were different way back then. A lot different.

JANICE:

(fighting for control) I'm sorry, but that's just not good enough!

BARB:

Hey, lady, we weren't even made citizens of our own country until 1960.

JANICE:

I know but . . .

BARB:

You don't know what it was like. I don't know what it was really like. None of us young people do. White people were always telling our people what to do, how to live, and if they didn't do it properly or broke the rules, they got punished. They got punished.

JANICE:

The poor Indians.

BARB:

Can the attitude, lady.

JANICE:

I am sick and tired of the "poor Indian" mentality. Somebody or something is always against them and I'm sick of it. I'm tired of explaining motives and drives that frankly I don't understand. If we are such a proud people then I find it hard to believe that every misfortune Indian people have suffered can be traced back to some malevolent white man. I'm to understand there's no such thing as a bad Indian. I'm sorry. But I don't buy it.

ANNE:

I suppose somebody somewhere had reasons for taking you away from us, and before I die I hope to understand them. But don't you for a moment think that it was because we didn't love you. When you were barely two months old, I got the fever. I got it bad, and I couldn't give you my milk. But you got sick, poor baby. Frank bundled the two of us up in the truck and drove us to town. We ran out of gas. Rather than let us walk in the cold or just sit there to wait, he pushed that truck the last three miles. Your father couldn't walk for the next five days because of you.

There is a long silence. Janice turns away and stands by the photo of herself and her father on the wall.

JANICE:

He did that?

Silence.

JANICE:

Please. *(she sits)* Please tell me. Then why did you give me up?

ANNE:

You weren't given up, you were taken.

Barb takes a deep breath.

BARB:

Brace yourself, it's really stupid. The stupidest thing I've ever heard. Times were hard around here, little or no money to be made. So Dad got this idea to join the army, regular money, and they take care of you. Sounded like a good idea.

JANICE:
He was a soldier?

BARB:
Uh huh. And there were rumours that Indians lost their status when they got discharged, so my dad, our dad, never told them he was Indian when he joined. He sent money home so Mom and you could eat. But the Indian agent became suspicious of a single mother living on the reserve and not on welfare. He called the Children's Aid and they sent an investigator who didn't find the home life . . .

ANNE:
. . . "suitable." My home wasn't suitable. What the heck do they know about what makes a home? I clothed you. I fed you. I loved you. Out here that was suitable. When that investigator woman stood there in my own kitchen not a foot from where you're sitting right now, when she stood there and said I'd been abandoned and I asked her what she was talking about anyways, and she said right to my face that I was a woman whose husband walked right out on her, I wanted to yell in her face, "Yes, I have a man and he didn't run out on me. He's a fine man gone to join the army to keep peace in this world and he sends me and his baby money." That's what I wanted to say to that . . . investigator woman from the Children's Aid. But I couldn't. Frank made me promise on the Bible not to, no matter what. He said it might get us in trouble. We got in trouble anyway. They took my little Grace right out of my arms and I never saw her again after that terrible day, God help me. They wouldn't even tell me where they took you. And poor Frank when he got back, and found out what happened, went drinking for four days. He'd never done that before. I almost lost it then but one of us had to be strong, so I was strong for the both of us.

BARB:
> After that Dad wouldn't talk about it, ever. Mom learned not to say your name around him. She never even put out that picture until after Dad died.

JANICE:
> That's it?

Silence.

JANICE:
> That's not even a reason. That wouldn't hold up in any court. And they call this a civilized country.

BARB:
> Welcome to the world of being Indian.

Janice approaches Anne.

JANICE:
> All of this, my life, because of some stupid woman's misunderstanding and a promise you made.

The emotion is getting to Janice. She begins to break.

JANICE:
> I have to go. I've got to get out of here.

She grabs her shoes and coat. Barb and Anne become alarmed.

BARB:
> Leave?! Just like that? You can't.

ANNE:
> Grace, please . . .

JANICE:
> You don't understand. I can't stay. I just can't.

BARB:
> Grace, Mom kinda expected you to stay for dinner.

She's been working real hard on everything and . . .

JANICE:
No, please. It isn't my place, my time. I don't belong here, Anne. I belong in Toronto now. I just had to meet you, put a face on my dream. I should go now.

ANNE:
Grace, wait!

Anne gets up and takes the pictures of Grace and Frank from the wall. She passes her fingers gently over the glass. She takes it to her eldest daughter and holds it out.

ANNE:
Grace. Take this. I want you to have it. Maybe it will help you to understand, and prove something to you. Look at him. No matter how many times you look at that man, you'll only see love.

JANICE:
I can't do that. I can't take it.

ANNE:
I have my memories of Frank. And now of you. And they're in colour. Take it. Frank would've given it to you.

Janice slowly takes it. She looks at the picture, keeping her eyes averted.

JANICE:
Thank you.

She puts it on the table as she begins to take off her moccasins.

BARB:
That's it?! You put your coat on and just walk out that door like it was anybody else's door but your own mother's? Do you know what this woman went through for you?

ANNE:
Barb, please.

BARB:
No, Mom. Grace, Janice, whatever the hell her name is, should know what's going on here. This woman is flying in relatives from all over for you. She would have spent every last cent of that five million looking for you. She's spent 35 years dreaming and waiting for you. And you're just going to walk out that door?

Janice looks down.

JANICE:
I'm sorry.

BARB:
Sorry don't cut it, Sister. I've lived in your shadow all my life, wondering if every time Mom and Dad looked at me they saw you. They never said your name but you were everywhere.

JANICE:
Consider yourself free now.

BARB:
No, it's not that easy. You're leaving me to pick up the pieces. Last time they *took* you out. This time you're walking out on your own. How do you think that's going to affect Mom?

JANICE:
Try to look at it from my side.

Janice holds out the moccasins for Barb to take.

JANICE:
I'm just not ready for this. Your moccasins.

There is silence between them.

BARB:
Take them, they're yours. We're millionaires now.

JANICE:
Thank you. I'll treasure them.

BARB:
Anytime, Sister.

Janice looks at them and then puts them on the picture.

ANNE:
You will come back soon, won't you?

JANICE:
Thank you for everything.

Anne watches from across the room. She opens her mouth to say something but nothing comes out. Instead she rushes to her daughter and hugs her tightly.

ANNE:
Baby. You're my baby Grace.

Anne brushes a strand of Janice's hair back from her face. She smiles up at her, and the lights within fade until they are in silhouette. Rodney enters, dragging his shovel. He looks at the portrait through the window.

RODNEY:
Ah, isn't that touching? Looks like there'll be three stockings over the fireplace for sure. This year, Santa came in a Saab. If I was sentimental I'd say all this was what Christmas was all about. It's a good thing I'm not. Forty-five minutes to the Grinch. And the nog. The sun has set over the lake and it's really starting to get cold, but I don't care cuz I feel warm inside and all is well with the world.

Janice walks down the driveway.

JANICE:
Ah, finished?

RODNEY:
Yep, it's all safe and sound. The car's up the road.
Figured I'd give the driveway a going over quickly
before I head home. No sense in you getting stuck
again. I see things are going well reunion-wise. (*beat*)
You've really made their Christmas. God, what a week—
millionaires, long lost relatives—has the makings of a
great made-for-tv movie. I'm waiting for Richard
Chamberlain to show up.

JANICE:
I'll never forget it. Uh, here.

She hands him a 20-dollar bill.

RODNEY:
What's that?

JANICE:
To thank you for your help.

RODNEY:
It's Christmas, don't be silly. Besides, we're practically
family.

JANICE:
Yes, well. Thank you, and have a good holiday.

Janice turns and starts walking towards the car.

RODNEY:
You're leaving? Now? They have all sorts of things
planned for you.

JANICE:
I know. And I hate to disappoint them, but I do have
other commitments. The Wirths are having a dinner
tonight. I have to be there.

RODNEY:
But what about Anne and Barb? It's not supposed to end this way. This should be a happy movie like *It's a Wonderful Life.*

JANICE:
Don't tell me about movies. I'm an entertainment lawyer. Movies are my life. Ironic, isn't it?

Rodney looks up and sees the silhouettes of the two women in the window.

RODNEY:
Grace . . .

JANICE:
Please call me Janice.

RODNEY:
Why did you come all the way out here, Janice?

JANICE:
Curiosity. There were some things I had to see and know. Both have been accomplished. It's time to go home.

RODNEY:
Anne thinks *this* is your home.

JANICE:
A couple of photographs, some tea, and a pair of moccasins don't make a home or a family. My family's waiting for me in London.

RODNEY:
But Anne's been waiting so long. She loves you.

JANICE:
She doesn't have the monopoly on love. I don't mean that to sound cruel but it's true. I do have other people I must see. God, I hope I don't break my neck in these shoes.

RODNEY:
When do you think you'll be back?

Janice looks up at the now empty window.

JANICE:
Oh, someday, I suppose. Goodbye, Rodney. And
Merry Christmas.

RODNEY:
Bye . . . Grace.

*Janice exits, carefully picking her way along. Rodney
watches her, depressed. He looks at the window, then off
towards home. He is deciding. A car starts up and drives
away.*

RODNEY:
I can go home now, I guess. Then again . . . Just go
home Rodney, like a good little boy. Make little
footyprints all the way to your front door. Beernog
awaits . . . Why did she have to do that? Look at that
tree. Oh geez . . .

He is stumped by indecision, then takes a deep breath.

RODNEY:
Life: the Creator's way of saying "impress me."

He picks up the tree and walks towards the house.

RODNEY:
God, I hate Christmas.

*Rodney braces himself, throws himself into a festive mood,
and sings from the heart.*

RODNEY:
"'Tis the season to be jolly, Fa la la la la, la la la la."

He enters the house.

The lights go down to a magical sparkling moonlight on the snow, and slowly fade to black.

THE END

About the Author

Drew Hayden Taylor has been called "one of Canada's leading Native dramatists" by the *Montreal Gazette*. His last play, *The Bootlegger Blues* (published in 1991), won the Canadian Authors Association Award for Drama. His first book, *Toronto at Dreamer's Rock* and *Education Is Our Right: Two One-Act Plays,* was published in 1990. The first play in that volume won Taylor a prestigious Chalmers Award in 1992 for the production by De-ba-jeh-mu-jig Theatre Group.

Drew Taylor is an Ojibway from the Curve Lake Reserve in Ontario. He writes drama for stage and screen and has contributed articles on Native arts and culture to many periodicals, including *Maclean's, Cinema Canada,* and *The Globe and Mail.* His play *Someday* first appeared as a short story on the front page of *The Globe and Mail*–the only piece of fiction ever to appear there–on Christmas Eve in 1990. He is currently working on a movie script for CBC-TV.